The
Religious Life
of
Theological Students

by
Benjamin B. Warfield

P U B L I S H I N G
P.O. BOX 817 • PHILLIPSBURG • NEW JERSEY 08865-0817

PUBLISHER'S NOTE

"The Religious Life of Theological Students" is one of fifty-nine articles in *The Selected Shorter Writings of Benjamin B. Warfield*, edited by John E. Meeter. It was delivered as an address by Dr. Warfield at the Autumn Conference at Princeton Theological Seminary, on October 4, 1911. It has been reprinted in its present form at the suggestion of members of the administration at several theological seminaries.

THE RELIGIOUS LIFE OF THEOLOGICAL STUDENTS

I am asked to speak to you on the religious life of the student of theology. I approach the subject with some trepidation. I think it the most important subject which can engage our thought. You will not suspect me, in saying this, to be depreciating the importance of the intellectual preparation of the student for the ministry. The importance of the intellectual preparation of the student for the ministry is the reason of the existence of our Theological Seminaries. Say what you will, do what you will, the ministry is a "learned profession"; and the man without learning, no matter with what other gifts he may be endowed, is unfit for its duties. But learning, though indispensable, is not the most indispensable thing for a minister. "Apt to teach" — yes, the minister must be "apt to teach"; and observe that what I say — or rather what Paul says — is "apt to *teach*." Not apt merely to exhort, to beseech, to appeal, to entreat; not even merely, to testify, to bear witness; but to *teach*. And teaching implies knowledge: he who teaches must know. Paul, in other words, requires of you, as we are perhaps learning not very felicitously to phrase it, "instructional," not merely "inspirational," service. But aptness to teach alone does not make a minister; nor is it his primary qualification. It is only one of a long list of requirements which Paul lays down as necessary to meet in him who aspires to this high office. And all the rest concern, not his intellectual, but his spiritual fitness. A minister must be learned, on pain of being utterly incompe-

1

tent for his work. But before and above being learned, a minister must be godly.

Nothing could be more fatal, however, than to set these two things over against one another. Recruiting officers do not dispute whether it is better for soldiers to have a right leg or a left leg: soldiers should have both legs. Sometimes we hear it said that ten minutes on your knees will give you a truer, deeper, more operative knowledge of God than ten hours over your books. "What!" is the appropriate response, "than ten hours over your books, on your knees?" Why should you turn from God when you turn to your books, or feel that you must turn from your books in order to turn to God? If learning and devotion are as antagonistic as that, then the intellectual life is in itself accursed, and there can be no question of a religious life for a student, even of theology. The mere fact that he is a student inhibits religion for him. That I am asked to speak to you on the religious life of the student of theology proceeds on the recognition of the absurdity of such antitheses. You are students of theology; and, just because you are students of theology, it is understood that you are religious men — especially religious men, to whom the cultivation of your religious life is a matter of the profoundest concern — of such concern that you will wish above all things to be warned of the dangers that may assail your religious life, and be pointed to the means by which you may strengthen and enlarge it. In your case there can be no "either — or" here — either a student or a man of God. You must be both.

Perhaps the intimacy of the relation between the work of a theological student and his religious life will nevertheless bear some emphasizing. Of course you do not think religion and study incompatible. But it is barely possible that there may be some among you who think of them too much apart — who are inclined to set their studies off to one side, and their religious life off to the other side, and to fancy that what is given to the one is taken from the other. No mistake could be more gross. Religion does not take a man away from his work; it sends him to his work with an added quality of devotion. We sing — do we not? —

Teach me, my God and King,
In all things Thee to see —
And what I do in anything,
To do it as for Thee.

If done t' obey Thy laws,
E'en servile labors shine:
Hallowed is toil, if this the cause,
The meanest work divine.

It is not just the way George Herbert wrote it. He puts, perhaps, a sharper point on it. He reminds us that a man may look at his work as he looks at a pane of glass — either seeing nothing but the glass, or looking straight through the glass to the wide heavens beyond. And he tells us plainly that there is nothing so mean but that the great words, "for thy sake," can glorify it:

A servant, with this clause,
Makes drudgery divine,
Who sweeps a room as for Thy laws,
Makes that, and the action, fine.

But the doctrine is the same, and it is the doctrine, the fundamental doctrine, of Protestant morality, from which the whole system of Christian ethics unfolds. It is the great doctrine of "vocation," the doctrine, to wit, that the best service we can offer to God is just to do our duty — our plain, homely duty, whatever that may chance to be. The Middle Ages did not think so; they cut a cleft between the religious and the secular life, and counseled him who wished to be religious to turn his back on what they called "the world," that is to say, not the wickedness that is in the world — "the world, the flesh and the devil," as we say — but the work-a-day world, that congeries of occupations which forms the daily task of men and women, who perform their duty to themselves and their fellowmen. Protestantism put an end to all that. As Professor Doumergue eloquently puts it, "Then Luther came, and, with still more consistency, Calvin, proclaiming the great idea of 'vocation,' an

3

idea and a word which are found in the languages of all the Protestant peoples — *Beruf, Calling, Vocation* — and which are lacking in the languages of the peoples of antiquity and of mediaeval culture. 'Vocation' — it is the call of God, addressed to every man, whoever he may be, to lay upon him a particular work, no matter what. And the calls, and therefore also the called, stand on a complete equality with one another. The burgomaster is God's burgomaster; the physician is God's physician; the merchant is God's merchant; the laborer is God's laborer. Every vocation, liberal, as we call it, or manual, the humblest and the vilest in appearance as truly as the noblest and the most glorious, is of divine right." Talk of the divine right of kings! Here is the divine right of every workman, no one of whom needs to be ashamed, if only he is an honest and good workman. "Only laziness," adds Professor Doumergue, "is ignoble, and while Romanism multiplies its mendicant orders, the Reformation banishes the idle from its towns."

Now, as students of theology your vocation is to study theology; and to study it diligently, in accordance with the apostolic injunction: "Whatsoever ye do, do it heartily, as to the Lord." It is precisely for this that you are students of theology; this is your "next duty," and the neglect of duty is not a fruitful religious exercise. Dr. Charles Hodge, in his delightful autobiographical notes, tells of Philip Lindsay, the most popular professor in the Princeton College of his day — a man sought by nearly every college in the Central States for its presidency — that "he told our class that we would find that one of the best preparations for death was a thorough knowledge of the Greek grammar." "This," comments Dr. Hodge, in his quaint fashion, "was his way of telling us that we ought to do our duty." Certainly, every man who aspires to be a religious man must begin by doing his duty, his obvious duty, his daily task, the particular work which lies before him to do at this particular time and place. If this work happens to be studying, then his religious life depends on nothing more fundamentally than on just studying. You might as well talk of a father who neglects his parental duties, of a son who fails in all the obligations of filial piety, of an artisan who systematically skimps his work and turns in a bad job, of a workman who is nothing better than an eye-servant, being religious men as of a student who does not study being a religious man. It cannot be: you cannot build up a religious life except you begin by performing faithfully your simple, daily duties. It is not the question whether you like these duties. You may think of your studies what you please. You may consider that you are singing precisely of them when you sing of "e'en servile labors," and of "the meanest work." But you must faithfully give yourselves to your studies, if you wish to be religious men. No religious character can be built up on the foundation of neglected duty.

There is certainly something wrong with the religious life of a theological student who does not study. But it does not quite follow that therefore everything is right with his religious life if he does study. It is possible to study — even to study theology — in an entirely secular spirit. I said a little while ago that what religion does is to send a man to his work with an added quality of devotion. In saying that, I meant the word "devotion" to be taken in both its senses — in the sense of "zealous application," and in the sense of "a religious exercise," as the Standard Dictionary phrases the two definitions. A truly religious man will study anything which it becomes his duty to study with "devotion" in both of these senses. That is what his religion does for him: it makes him do his duty, do it thoroughly, do it "in the Lord." But in the case of many branches of study, there is nothing in the topics studied which tends directly to feed the religious life, or to set in movement the religious emotions, or to call out specifically religious reactions. If we study them "in the Lord," that is only because we do it "for his sake," on the principle which makes "sweeping a room" an act of worship. With theology it is not so. In all its branches alike, theology has as its unique end to make God known: the student of theology is brought by his daily task into the presence of God, and is kept there. Can a religious man stand in the presence of God, and not worship? It is possible, I have said, to study even theology in a purely secular spirit. But surely that is possible only for an irreligious man, or at least for an unreligious man. And here I place in your

5

hands at once a touchstone by which you may discern your religious state, and an instrument for the quickening of your religious life. Do you prosecute your daily tasks as students of theology as "religious exercises"? If you do not, look to yourselves: it is surely not all right with the spiritual condition of that man who can busy himself daily with divine things, with a cold and impassive heart. If you do, rejoice. But in any case, see that you do! And that you do it ever more and more abundantly. Whatever you may have done in the past, for the future make all your theological studies "religious exercises." This is the great rule for a rich and wholesome religious life in a theological student. Put your heart into your studies; do not merely occupy your mind with them, but put your heart into them. They bring you daily and hourly into the very presence of God; his ways, his dealing with men, the infinite majesty of his Being form their very subject-matter. Put the shoes from off your feet in this holy presence!

We are frequently told, indeed, that the great danger of the theological student lies precisely in his constant contact with divine things. They may come to seem common to him, because they are customary. As the average man breathes the air and basks in the sunshine without ever a thought that it is God in his goodness who makes his sun to rise on him, though he is evil, and sends rain to him, though he is unjust; so you may come to handle even the furniture of the sanctuary with never a thought above the gross earthly materials of which it is made. The words which tell you of God's terrible majesty or of his glorious goodness may come to be mere words to you — Hebrew and Greek words, with etymologies, and inflections, and connections in sentences. The reasonings which establish to you the mysteries of his saving activities may come to be to you mere logical paradigms, with premises and conclusions, fitly framed, no doubt, and triumphantly cogent, but with no further significance to you than their formal logical conclusiveness. God's stately steppings in his redemptive processes may become to you a mere series of facts of history, curiously interplaying to the production of social and religious conditions, and pointing mayhap to an issue which we may shrewdly conjecture: but much like other facts occurring in time and space, which may come to your notice. It *is* your great danger. But it is your great danger, only because it is your great privilege. Think of what your privilege is when your greatest danger is that the great things of religion may become common to you! Other men, oppressed by the hard conditions of life, sunk in the daily struggle for bread perhaps, distracted at any rate by the dreadful drag of the world upon them and the awful rush of the world's work, find it hard to get time and opportunity so much as to pause and consider whether there be such things as God, and religion, and salvation from the sin that compasses them about and holds them captive. The very atmosphere of your life is these things; you breathe them in at every pore; they surround you, encompass you, press in upon you from every side. It is all in danger of becoming common to you! God forgive you, you are in danger of becoming weary of God!

Do you know what this danger is? Or, rather, let us turn the question — are you alive to what your privileges are? Are you making full use of them? Are you, by this constant contact with divine things, growing in holiness, becoming every day more and more men of God? If not, you are hardening! And I am here today to warn you to take seriously your theological study, not merely as a duty, done for God's sake and therefore made divine, but as a religious exercise, itself charged with religious blessing to you; as fitted by its very nature to fill all your mind and heart and soul and life with divine thoughts and feelings and aspirations and achievements. You will never prosper in your religious life in the Theological Seminary until your work in the Theological Seminary becomes itself to you a religious exercise out of which you draw every day enlargement of heart, elevation of spirit, and adoring delight in your Maker and your Savior.

I am not counseling you, you will observe, to make your theological studies your sole religious exercises. They are religious exercises of the most rewarding kind; and your religious life will very much depend upon your treating them as such. But there are other religious exercises demanding your punctual attention which cannot be neglected without the gravest dam-

7

age to your religious life. I refer particularly now to the stated formal religious meetings of the Seminary. I wish to be perfectly explicit here, and very emphatic. No man can withdraw himself from the stated religious services of the community of which he is a member, without serious injury to his personal religious life. It is not without significance that the apostolic writer couples together the exhortations, "to hold fast the confession of our hope, that it waver not," and "to forsake not the assembling of ourselves together." When he commands us not to forsake "the assembling of ourselves together," he has in mind, as the term he employs shows, the stated, formal assemblages of the community, and means to lay upon the hearts and consciences of his readers their duty to the church of which they are the supports, as well as their duty to themselves. And when he adds, "As the custom of some is," he means to put a lash into his command. We can see his lip curl as he says it. Who are these people, who are so vastly strong, so supremely holy, that they do not need the assistance of the common worship for themselves; and who, being so strong and holy, will not give their assistance to the common worship?

Needful as common worship is, however, for men at large, the need of it for men at large is as nothing compared with its needfulness for a body of young men situated as you are. You are gathered together here for a religious purpose, in preparation for the highest religious service which can be performed by men — the guidance of others in the religious life; and shall you have everything else in common except worship? You are gathered together here, separated from your homes and all that home means; from the churches in which you have been brought up, and all that church fellowship means; from all the powerful natural influences of social religion — and shall you not yourselves form a religious community, with its own organic religious life and religious expression? I say it deliberately, that a body of young men, living apart in a community-life, as you are and must be living, cannot maintain a healthy, full, rich religious life individually, unless they are giving organic expression to their religious life as a community in frequent stated diets of common worship. Nothing can take the place of this common organic worship of the community as a community, at its stated seasons, and as a regular function of the corporate life of the community. Without it you cease to be a religious community and lack that support and stay, that incitement and spur, that comes to the individual from the organic life of the community of which he forms a part.

In my own mind, I am quite clear that in an institution like this the whole body of students should come together, both morning and evening, every day, for common prayer; and should join twice on every Sabbath in formal worship. Without at least this much common worship I do not think the institution can preserve its character as a distinctively religious institution — an institution whose institutional life is primarily a religious one. And I do not think that the individual students gathered here can, with less full expression of the organic religious life of the institution, preserve the high level of religious life on which, as students of theology, they ought to live. You will observe that I am not merely exhorting you "to go to church." "Going to church" is in any case good. But what I am exhorting you to do is to go to your own church — to give your presence and active religious participation to every stated meeting for worship of the institution as an institution. Thus you will do your part to give to the institution an organic religious life, and you will draw out from the organic religious life of the institution a support and inspiration for your own personal religious life which you can get nowhere else, and which you can cannot afford to miss — if, that is, you have a care to your religious quickening and growth. To be an active member of a living religious body is the condition of healthy religious functioning.

I trust you will not tell me that the stated religious exercises of the Seminary are too numerous, or are wearying. That would only be to betray the low ebb of your own religious vitality. The feet of him whose heart is warm with religious feeling turn of themselves to the sanctuary, and carry him with joyful steps to the house of prayer. I am told that there are some students who do not find themselves in a prayerful mood in the early hours of a winter morning; and are much too tired at the close of a hard day's work to pray, and therefore do not find it profitable to attend prayers in the late afternoon: who think the preaching at the regular service on Sabbath morning dull and uninteresting, and who do not find Christ at the Sabbath afternoon conference. Such things I seem to have heard before; and yours will be an exceptional pastorate, if you do not hear something very like them, before you have been in a pastorate six months. Such things meet you every day on the street; they are the ordinary expression of the heart which is dulled or is dulling to the religious appeal. They are not hopeful symptoms among those whose life should be lived on the religious heights. No doubt, those who minister to you in spiritual things should take them to heart. And you who are ministered to must take them to heart, too. And let me tell you straightout that the preaching you find dull will no more seem dull to you if you faithfully obey the Master's precept: "Take heed how ye hear"; that if you do not find Christ in the conference room it is because you do not take him there with you; that, if after an ordinary day's work you are too weary to unite with your fellows in closing the day with common prayer, it is because the impulse to prayer is weak in your heart. If there is no fire in the pulpit it falls to you to kindle it in the pews. No man can fail to meet with God in the sanctuary if he takes God there with him.

How easy it is to roll the blame of our cold hearts over upon the shoulders of our religious leaders! It is refreshing to observe how Luther, with his breezy good sense, dealt with complaints of lack of attractiveness in his evangelical preachers. He had not sent them out to please people, he said, and their function was not to interest or to entertain; their function was to teach the saving truth of God, and, if they did that, it was frivolous for people in danger of perishing for want of the truth to object to the vessel in which it was offered to them. When the people of Torgau, for instance, wished to dismiss their pastors, because, they said, their voices were too weak to fill the churches, Luther simply responded, "That's an old song: better have some difficulty in hearing the gospel than no difficulty at all in hearing what is very far from the gospel."

"People cannot have their ministers exactly as they wish," he declares again, "they should thank God for the pure word," and not demand St. Augustines and St. Ambroses to preach it to them. If a pastor pleases the Lord Jesus and is faithful to him, — there is none so great and mighty but he ought to be pleased with him, too. The point, you see, is that men who are hungry for the truth and get it ought not to be exigent as to the platter in which it is served to them. And they will not be. But why should we appeal to Luther? Have we not the example of our Lord Jesus Christ? Are we better than he? Surely, if ever there was one who might justly plead that the common worship of the community had nothing to offer him it was the Lord Jesus Christ. But every Sabbath found him seated in his place among the worshipping people, and there was no act of stated worship which he felt himself entitled to discard. Even in his most exalted moods, and after his most elevating experiences, he quietly took his place with the rest of God's people, sharing with them in the common worship of the community. Returning from that great baptismal scene, when the heavens themselves were rent to bear him witness that he was well pleasing to God; from the searching trials of the wilderness, and from that first great tour in Galilee, prosecuted, as we are expressly told, "in the power of the Spirit"; he came back, as the record tells, "to Nazareth, where he had been brought up, and" — so proceeds the amazing narrative — "he entered, as his custom was, into the synagogue, on the Sabbath day." "As his custom was!" Jesus Christ made it his habitual practice to be found in his place on the Sabbath day at the stated place of worship to which he belonged. "It is a reminder," as Sir William Robertson Nicoll well insists, "of the truth which, in our fancied spirituality, we are apt to forget — that the holiest personal life can scarcely afford to dispense with stated forms of devotion, and that the regular public worship of the church, for all its local imperfections and dullness, is a divine provision for sustaining the individual soul." "We cannot afford to be wiser than our Lord in this matter. If any one could have pled that his spiritual experience was so lofty that it did not require public worship, if any one might have felt that the consecration

11

and communion of his personal life exempted him from what ordinary mortals needed, it was Jesus. But he made no such plea. Sabbath by Sabbath even he was found in the place of worship, side by side with God's people, not for the mere sake of setting a good example, but for deeper reasons. Is it reasonable, then, that any of us should think we can safely afford to dispense with the pious custom of regular participation with the common worship of our locality?" Is it necessary for me to exhort those who would fain be like Christ, to see to it that they are imitators of him in this?

But not even with the most assiduous use of the corporate expressions of the religious life of the community have you reached the foundation-stone of your piety. That is to be found, of course, in your closets, or rather in your hearts, in your private religious exercises, and in your intimate religious aspirations. You are here as theological students; and if you would be religious men, you must do your duty as theological students; you must find daily nourishment for your religious life in your theological studies; you must enter fully into the organic religious life of the community of which you form a part. But to do all this you must keep the fires of religious life burning brightly in your heart; in the inmost core of your being, you must be men of God. Time would fail me, if I undertook to outline with any fulness the method of the devout life. Every soul seeking God honestly and earnestly finds him, and, in finding him, finds the way to him. One hint I may give you, particularly adapted to you as students for the ministry: Keep always before your mind the greatness of your calling, that is to say, these two things: the immensity of the task before you, the infinitude of the resources at your disposal. I think it has not been idly said, that if we face the tremendous difficulty of the work before us, it will certainly throw us back upon our knees; and if we worthily gauge the power of the gospel committed to us, that will certainly keep us on our knees. I am led to single out this particular consideration, because it seems to me that we have fallen upon an age in which we very greatly need to recall ourselves to the seriousness of life and its issues, and to the seriousness of our calling as ministers to life. Sir

Oliver Lodge informs us that "men of culture are not bothering," nowadays, "about their sins, much less about their punishment," and Dr. Johnston Ross preaches us a much needed homily from that text on the "lightheartedness of the modern religious quest." In a time like this, it is perhaps not strange that careful observers of the life of our Theological Seminaries tell us that the most noticeable thing about it is a certain falling off from the intense seriousness of outlook by which students of theology were formerly characterized. Let us hope it is not true. If it were true, it would be a great evil; so far as it is true, it is a great evil. I would call you back to this seriousness of outlook, and bid you cultivate it, if you would be men of God now, and ministers who need not be ashamed hereafter. Think of the greatness of the minister's calling; the greatness of the issues which hang on your worthiness or your unworthiness for its high functions; and determine once for all that with God's help you will be worthy. "God had but one Son," says Thomas Goodwin, "and he made him a minister." "None but he who made the world," says John Newton, "can make a minister" — that is, a minister who is worthy.

You can, of course, be a minister of a sort, and not be God-made. You can go through the motions of the work, and I shall not say that your work will be in vain — for God is good and who knows by what instruments he may work his will of good for men? Helen Jackson pictures far too common an experience when she paints the despair of one whose sowing, though not unfruitful for others, bears no harvest in his own soul.

> O teacher, then I said, thy years,
> Are they not joy? each word that issueth
> From out thy lips, doth it return to bless
> Thine own heart manyfold?

Listen to the response:

> I starve with hunger treading out their corn,
> I die of travail while their souls are born.

She does not mean it in quite the evil part in which I am reading it. But what does Paul mean when he utters that terrible warning: "Lest when I have preached to others, I myself should be a castaway?" And there is an even more dreadful contingency. It is our Savior himself who tells us that it is possible to compass sea and land to make one proselyte, and when we have made him to make him twofold more a child of hell than we are ourselves. And will we not be in awful peril of making our proselytes children of hell if we are not ourselves children of heaven? Even physical waters will not rise above their source: the spiritual floods are even less tractable to our commands. There is no mistake more terrible than to suppose that activity in Christian work can take the place of depth of Christian affections.

This is the reason why many good men are shaking their heads a little today over a tendency which they fancy they see increasing among our younger Christian workers to restless activity at the apparent expense of depth of spiritual culture. Activity, of course, is good: surely in the cause of the Lord we should run and not be weary. But not when it is substituted for inner religious strength. We cannot get along without our Marthas. But what shall we do when, through all the length and breadth of the land, we shall search in vain for a Mary? Of course the Marys will be as little admired by the Marthas today as of yore. "Lord," cried Martha, "dost thou not care that my sister hath left me to serve alone?" And from that time to this the cry has continually gone up against the Marys that they waste the precious ointment which might have been given to the poor, when they pour it out to God, and are idle when they sit at the Master's feet. A minister, high in the esteem of the churches, is even quoted as declaring — not confessing, mind you, but publishing abroad as something in which he gloried — that he has long since ceased to pray: he *works.* "Work and pray" is no longer, it seems, to be the motto of at least ministerial life. It is to be all work and no praying; the only prayer that is prevailing, we are told, with the same cynicism with which we are told that God is on the side of the largest battalions — is just work. You will say this is an extreme case. Thank God, it is. But in the tendencies of our modern life, which all make for ceaseless — I had almost said thoughtless, meaningless — activity, have a care that it does not become your case; or that your case — even now — may not have at least some resemblance to it. Do you pray? How much do you pray? How much do you love to pray? What place in your life does the "still hour," alone with God, take? I am sure that if you once get a true glimpse of what the ministry of the cross is, for which you are preparing, and of what you, as men preparing for this ministry, should be, you will pray, Lord, who is sufficient for these things, your heart will cry; and your whole soul will be wrung with the petition: Lord, make me sufficient for these things. Old Cotton Mather wrote a great little book once, to serve as a guide to students for the ministry. The not very happy title which he gave it is *Manductio ad Ministerium*. But by a stroke of genius he added a sub-title which is more significant. And this is the sub-title he added: *The angels preparing to sound the trumpets*. That is what Cotton Mather calls you, students for the ministry: the angels, preparing to sound the trumpets! Take the name to yourselves, and live up to it. Give your days and nights to living up to it! And then, perhaps, when you come to sound the trumpets the note will be pure and clear and strong, and perchance may pierce even to the grave and wake the dead.